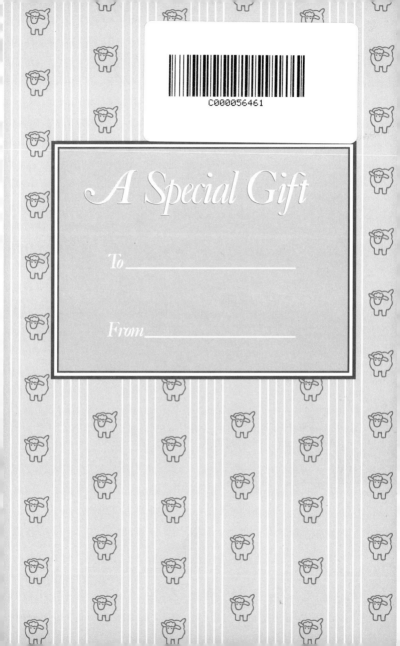

A Special Gift

To _____

From _____

Before Your Baby Comes

Books for Adults by William Coleman

Before Your Baby Comes

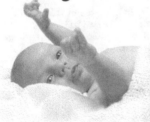

PARENTS' THOUGHTS ON MOTHERHOOD

William & Patricia Coleman

BETHANY HOUSE PUBLISHERS

Minneapolis, Minnesota 55438

Published by Bethany House Publishers
A Ministry of Bethany Fellowship, Inc.
11300 Hampshire Avenue South
Minneapolis, Minnesota 55438

Printed in the United States of America.

**Library of Congress
Cataloging-in-Publication Data**

Coleman, William L.
    Before your baby comes : parent's thoughts on
motherhood / William and Patricia Coleman.
        p.   cm.

    1. Motherhood.   I. Coleman, Patricia.
II. Title.
HQ759.C69   1995
306.874'3—dc20   95–20774
ISBN 1–55661–564–7   CIP

To Nolan Michael Cooney

WILLIAM AND PATRICIA COLEMAN
have been married for more than thirty
years and are the parents of three grown
children. Long recognized as outstanding
communicators on family relationships,
they combine in this book Bill's writing experience and Pat's practical advice. Bill is
the well-known author of more that thirty
Bethany House books on a variety of topics.

Contents

Introduction to Parenting

We are forever indebted to Mary. When she came into our lives, we knew very little about parenting. But from the first time we held her in our arms and took her to our small mobile home in Indiana, Mary started her own "hands-on" clinic on parenthood.

Daily and nightly, this newborn conducted classes. She taught us how to change diapers and re-change them five minutes later. We were assigned to midnight floor-walking and trained in the fine art of burping. We were instructed how to interpret her different kinds of cries: urgent, tired, hungry, fussy, wet, cutesy, pleading, and, of course, the super-wail— her way of reminding us who was in charge.

She gave lessons in trust, tenderness, smiling, cooing, loving, and wrapping adults around her little finger. Mary was a master teacher sent from above to train fledgling, inexperienced parents. Later Jim and June came along to help us complete our graduate courses.

Having a child is one of the Lord's richest blessings. We look back with great satisfaction and thankfulness to Him. Nothing has exceeded the pure joy of having our own babies. The thoughts expressed in the following chapters are our separate and joint attempts to pay back a small portion of the many gifts we've received from our firstborn daughter.

To Mary, and to new parents everywhere, we recommend you latch onto a rocking chair, a helpful book, a blood relative, and a small bottle of aspirin. You're in for one exciting ride!

Love,
Bill and Pat Coleman
(otherwise known as Mom and Dad
or Grandma and Grandpa)

The Best News

We tried to stay calm and not shout too loudly. We tried to keep our cool and not make a scene, but our hearts were on the ceiling.

You told us you'd dreamed about the day when you could tell your husband you were pregnant. Then you said you wanted to see the looks on your parents' faces when they heard the news.

Nothing could have moved us more. Our grown, educated, married daughter wanted to see the smiles on our faces and the sparkle in our eyes. You certainly know how to make two frosty-haired adults feel loved and wanted. Thanks for telling us right away.

We are thrilled to feel so much a part of this big event. We think children and grandparents make a great combo. For years we've been looking for an excuse to go to the circus. And what good is a zoo without a little person tagging alongside holding your index finger?

We are confident that you'll be a great mom. Your decision to curtail your career so you could have a child shows how much you and Gerry want a family. You have a good concept of what really counts in life.

We promise to keep in touch. We also promise to pray. God will want to hear how the pregnancy's going, and He'll want to know about all of your needs.

Promises to Keep

*G*randparenting is new to us, so you'll have to excuse us for being amateurs. We've had some good role modeling, but the rest we'll have to learn on the job.

If you're going to trust us to grandparent your child, we think you should have some idea of what to expect. Here's part of the contribution we want to make:

As grandparents we promise:

- To be a significant presence so your child will know there are a couple of old people who think she or he is terrific.
- We promise to baby-sit enough to be

helpful and probably more than that.

- We promise to correct your child, but only enough for the child's safety and to protect our dishes. We intend to be the "candy and cookie people" and let you be the "parental police."

- We promise to button our lips when you correct your child. Discipline has to be at your pace and in your style.

- We promise to make our home child-friendly. Going to grandparents' house shouldn't be a boring experience. We plan to keep the toy box and cookie jar full, fresh, and accessible.

- We promise to supply more hugs than all-star wrestlers. We also promise to tussle on the floor and give plenty of piggyback rides.

- We promise to carry the baby on our shoulders so she can see far away. We won't even complain when her ice cream cone drips on our foreheads.

- We promise to read aloud, listen to stories, help open wrappers, and show how to blow bubbles.

- We promise to go to the Platte River

and watch Sandhill cranes and to Pintail Preserve when ducks and geese fly in. We won't let our grandchild grow up without listening to frogs and seeing the raccoon and opossum in our backyard.

- We promise to take our grandchild places as soon as you give the okay. Parks, nature walks, movies, parades, zoos, circuses, baseball games, church events, fairs, and magic shows are just a few of the fun outings we have planned.

- We promise to talk to the Lord about our grandchild. We'll ask Him to send an especially sharp guardian angel.

- We promise to take good care of ourselves. This child is going to need grandparents for a long time.

We better quit. If the job description gets any longer, we'll have to take an early retirement and come on full-time!

One more promise. We will love our grandchild's parents with all our hearts.

Already a Good Mother

Even before your baby is born you've made the ultimate loving decision. You're willing to make whatever sacrifices are necessary to be a good mother.

Gone are the
    caffeine
    harmful chemicals
    late nights.
Here to stay are
    extra veggies
    proper exercise
    plenty of rest.
You don't want to picture this unborn

baby as a bundle of nerves, fidgeting, flinching, and shaking in your womb. Let the little babe have nine months to develop well before entering this chaotic world. Your child will be exposed to the hectic highways of life soon enough. Do all you can now to ensure the comfort, strength, and peace that can be found only inside the body of a loving mother.

Too many unborn babies suffer the effects of toxic waste, smoke, alcohol, drugs, and other contaminants while they're still helpless victims. Pity the millions of babies who must struggle to overcome illnesses and addictions contracted unnecessarily in the womb.

We heard about the note Gerry left by your bed after you resigned from your job, reminding you that you didn't give up your job to "get things done." You chose to stay home to take care of yourself and your baby in preparation for giving birth.

Mothering is too important a role to do haphazardly. Being mothered is a little one's introduction to life. All that you do, most of which your baby will never remem-

19

ber, are continuous acts of love by someone who cares from the depths of her heart and soul.

God gave mothers special wisdom. Smart mothers put that wisdom to work early and continue to lean on it through the years.

Here's to Your Good Health

*P*regnancy is a normal, healthy bodily function; but it is complex enough to justify continual, careful monitoring throughout the nine months.

I'm glad you have a doctor/midwife team in whom you have confidence. The doctor will initially give you a thorough exam, including blood tests and urinalysis. Monthly he or she will check your weight gain, urine, and blood pressure reading. As the months progress your doctor will also check the fetal heartbeat, the size and position of your uterus, the position of the baby, and look for swelling of your hands and feet.

Your doctor will want you to report exposure to German measles or other infectious diseases. He'll also tell you if anything in your medical history requires special attention or testing.

It's helpful to make a list of questions to ask during your prenatal check-ups, and don't hesitate to call the doctor's office between visits.

Your doctor will tell you what your weight gain should be throughout the pregnancy. I'm happy to see how carefully you're following a prescribed diet plan. You're doing a good job of eating all the right things to nourish yourself and your baby. You've shown great discipline in drinking extra liquids and avoiding certain foods. Your unborn baby is building new tissues, and your cells need to be replenished as they are being drained by the baby. Keep eating those types of foods that help your kidneys and intestines function efficiently.

You were smart to leave the house when

the interior was being painted. You're very prudent about checking with your doctor before using household cleaning products or insecticides. If you do use any chemicals, avoid aerosol cans and make sure there's proper ventilation.

Another caution: "No drug can be assumed to be harmless if you are pregnant." Even aspirin. Since the baby is nourished through the placenta, what you intake affects him or her. Again, ask the doctor.

One more: Avoid extremely hot baths, especially during the early months.

Since you have been in exercise classes for several years, you'll be able to continue with exercises for pregnant women.

Yes, it's a lot to think about, but you're doing well!

Morning Sickness

*I*t's no fun when the mention of food, smells from the kitchen, or opening the refrigerator door make you run for the bathroom. Normally, your discomfort—and sometimes misery—will last only a couple of months. Some fortunate mothers-to-be never experience nausea, while some mothers with twins tell me they had morning sickness even up to the ninth month.

Somehow the developing baby seems to get enough nutrition during this time. If you get extra rest, eliminate stress, and try to eat and drink as you are able, all should go well.

24

Here are a few tips I've found that can help you cope:

1. Aim for good nutrition so that the foods you can retain will keep you and the baby strong. Experiment with all kinds of fruits, vegetables, meats, and breads to see what your stomach can handle. The prenatal vitamins your doctor prescribed will help supplement your dietary needs during this time.

2. Try all kinds of fluids. Sometimes they are easier than solids to digest. Milk shakes, fruit and vegetable juices, and some soups may taste good to you.

3. Eating lots of small snacks during the day rather than three large meals will probably make you feel better. It helps to keep something in your stomach at all times. I found crackers was all I could keep down some days.

4. First thing in the morning was the worst time for me. If you find that to be true for you, try keeping a few crackers by your bed to eat before you get up. Also eat something at bedtime so you won't wake up with an empty stomach.

25

5. Extra sleep and relaxation will help. Your dad had to fill in at our house getting the children dressed and fed in the morning. Your body needs some extra pampering right now.

Your nausea appears to be normal, and in short order you should be feeling fine again.

Encouraging news: This, too, will pass!

Jumping for Joy

ave you ever wondered what exactly your baby is doing inside the womb? At first you might think your son or daughter must be sleeping round the clock and sort of passing the time away. But soon the quiet stage ends and the "activity" stage begins.

Baby starts to move around with considerable force. Is it punching or kicking you feel? Maybe baby has begun an exercise routine. Could these be fetal aerobics? Maybe babies do jumping jacks or push-ups.

We'd like to consider another possibility. Could it be your baby is actually jumping for joy? Don't reject this idea until you've taken time to weigh the evidence. Jumping for joy isn't unheard of and it's far from impossible.

The baby in your womb has a great deal to be happy about. Your baby's mother gives excellent care. She gets plenty of rest, eats well, and has a fantastic attitude. Mother talks and sings to baby while father adds his reassuring voice and words of encouragement.

Not much environmental clutter gets into womb world. No cigarette smoke, no alcohol, and a minimum of industrial fumes. Generally baby is free from any foreign, harmful matter that might otherwise clog its days and nights.

The Bible gives us a glimpse of Elizabeth's pregnancy when her cousin, Mary the mother of Jesus, came to see her. When Mary said hello to Elizabeth, the baby "leaped for joy" inside Elizabeth's womb.

There was probably some special miracle involved in that particular account of baby jumping, but baby conceiving, womb development, and birth are always surrounded with miracles whether we recognize them or not.

There's no way we can prove it. We can't hook up electronic equipment to check the developing baby for joy jumping and get back to you with the printout.

But scientific evidence probably isn't very good at measuring joy.

All we know is that joy jumping
 could happen
 should happen
 has happened
 might happen again.

We also know your baby has a great deal to be joyful about. Go ahead. Give your baby the benefit of the doubt. Your little one isn't punching you in the stomach. Your son or daughter is jumping for joy.

Your Love for
Little Ones

Whlie I was in college I worked part-time at a large real estate firm. One of the hundred or so employees was a bright, independent woman who was very much in charge of her own life. That is, until she arrived at work one day and announced that she was pregnant. The confident, goal-centered lady looked stunned. Having a baby wasn't one of the stepping stones on her path to success and happiness.

To her credit, she made the adjustment.

By the time her baby arrived, she was tickled at the prospect. She went home to make delivery and I never saw her at work again.

For some mothers the adjustment is too much. They never imagined themselves as gentle mothers rocking a baby to sleep. They never pictured themselves bragging about a child's first tooth.

You have a big advantage here, Mary. All of your life we could picture you with your own children. You always had mothering, caring instincts. You were drawn to little tykes, complete with the patience of a saint. You hovered over your little brother and sister like a mother hen.

Whether we were visiting another family, playing in the park, or hanging out at the church nursery, you immediately "looked after" the little ones. You fetched bottles, grabbed pacifiers, collected toys. And as soon as you were old enough you were holding a toddler, almost as big as yourself, tight in your arms, parked on your extended hip.

By the time you left home for the rigors of a kindergarten education, your nickname was "Mother Mary." Like a detector searching for metal, your beeper went off whenever you were near an infant.

For many mothers the draw is not natural. They are not irresistibly moved toward a small cooing bundle or a wobbly-kneed kid with a beach bucket. But once they see their own edition of loving humanity, their coolness usually turns into a warm glow.

Your husband is vital to you as are your relatives, your friends, and your church. You seem to have your priorities in good order. But inside your heart there has always been a cradle-shaped vacuum. And now that cradle is filled.

Ultrasound

The first time I saw a young woman studying an ultrasound picture of her unborn child, I could see the thrill in her glowing face. It was like a miracle on top of a miracle. She actually held a picture before she held her baby.

The procedure for this scientific wonder is relatively simple. The mother-to-be lies on a table and either a scanner is passed over her abdomen or a probe is inserted inside her. The instruments record echoes of sound waves as they bounce off parts of the baby's body. These sound waves show up in patterns of light on a TV-like viewing screen. An image of the baby appears on the screen.

A level one ultrasound is performed primarily to evaluate age and growth of the baby and to see the position and determine if multiple births are suspected. A more detailed or level two ultrasound is used if the doctor suspects a condition that needs monitoring or to answer any questions he or she may have.

With the help of a trained person, you may be able to see the beating heart, the curve of the spine, the head, arms, and legs. You may even be able to see your baby sucking his thumb. Sometimes, if the baby is positioned right, the sex can be surmised, though this isn't 100% reliable. Your doctor will ask you whether or not you want to know the baby's sex before the birth.

Some doctors use ultrasound routinely and others use it rarely. Talk it over at your next appointment if you have any questions. There is no known risk to the baby and no pain for the mother (except the discomfort of a full bladder with the transab-dominal exam).

A touch of technology, an ultrasound, like much of science, can be a valuable link between you and the child you love.

What's in a Name?

*P*utting a label on your own baby is a big deal. Even if you decide on a short or a common name, it still has to be weighed, thought out, and mulled over carefully.

When parents assign a name, there's a special meaning behind it. To them it says something unique about their child. Names aren't given thoughtlessly.

Sometimes names bring to mind thoughts of other people. It might represent an aunt or a grandfather. Maybe it makes you think of a famous person. We thought about giving you another name, but we knew everyone would think of the movie star by that name when they heard it.

Start off by asking what you want the name to say to you. It needs to have a satisfying, fulfilling sound to the parent who gave it. Make yourselves happy.

Most people select one of the top twenty names of the day. They want their child's name to be contemporary and up-to-date, so he will fit in well. Others prefer a unique name to give the child a particular identity. Some parents study books on the meanings of names to help them choose just the right one.

Don't, however, just make yourselves happy. Try to imagine how your child will live with this title. Will the child suffer because of some strange name she has to defend all her life?

What kind of nickname will this name have? Many of us aren't called by our given names. Friends and relatives frequently turn names into twisted blades and keep sticking us with them.

Also, ask yourself if you really want an alternative spelling. It might look cute to add an "i" at the end or throw in an extra "d," but remember children become adults and will have to spell their names this way all of their lives, every time.

It's fun to name a son after his father, but the "Junior" appendage can get in the way. For much of his life he won't be called by his father's name but merely "Junior." (And then again, I know a fine person who was given the real first name of Junior. He was called Hank.)

The boxer, George Foreman, named all five of his sons "George." When his wife says, "It's time for dinner, George," everyone comes.

Choosing a child's name is a rare privilege God extends only so often in our lives. It's worth all the wrestling we go through. Pick a name with a good ring to it and a satisfying image the child will be proud to carry around.

Nerves and Networking

*Y*our mother made a science out of being pregnant. She bought and borrowed books, read articles, and toured the hospital. You've done all that and more. We like to feel confident when something this monumental comes along.

But even with all your new knowledge and expectations, don't be surprised if you feel a little nervous. This is a new adventure. Most parents wonder if they're up to the task, but every conscientious mother who's willing to learn, ask questions, and adapt to the changes manages to pull it off. Love for an infant, who totally needs and depends on us, gives us courage and calls up strength we never thought we had.

Apprehension is normal. Parenting is an awesome responsibility as well as an exhilarating adventure. Most satisfying accomplishments come with a bit of built-in fear. That's part of the joy. Parenting is hard, but let's not miss out on the blessings simply because it's difficult.

Smart parents maintain a network. They have a special list of phone numbers that includes the numbers of doctors, mothers, fathers, sisters, friends, pastors, and even brothers. When doubts and fears do their dirty work, wise new mothers head for the phone. They even call collect, if necessary.

Networking reduces the uncertainty. Sometimes you'll need to know what to do, and just as often you'll need someone to affirm you. You'll need someone to say it's normal for babies to cry. Or someone you can ask if the baby really smiled or if it was only gas. You'll need someone you can ask to come over and hold a fussy baby for an hour so you can sleep. There is much to learn with the first baby, and the responsibility of caring for a tiny life can be overwhelming.

Don't go solo. Aloneness only causes fears to flourish. Friendly voices, gentle advice, and assurance from those with experience can chase the shadows of insecurity away.

It's all right to say, "I'm apprehensive." We can all deal with that. Serious problems arise when we drop down a notch and say, "I'm apprehensive; there must be something wrong with me." Don't entertain that thought. Once in a while we all get scared. That's the way we're made.

After all, they say every good host is a little jittery,
    every good speaker is nervous,
    every good artist takes some risks,
    every good student tries something new.
And every parent is apprehensive. It comes with the territory.

Round-the-Clock Care

*O*ne of the biggest shocks for new parents is that a baby requires care twenty-four hours a day.

This round-the-clock care isn't like baby-sitting, where at midnight or 2:00 A.M. the baby-sitter parts company with her little charge. Baby then goes on with his normal routine while the baby-sitter retreats to her home and sleeps until 11:30 on Saturday morning.

The reality of parenthood was best expressed to us one day when a new mom looked at us with a totally spaced-out gaze and moaned, "I never realized that I'd never

42

get any relief from caring for the baby. She needs me around the clock."

Don't be surprised.

Don't panic.

Don't reject help.

If you choose to nurse, the situation will be more intense. A nursing mother can't hand a crying infant to her husband at 3:00 A.M. and say, "The baby's hungry."

But with the exception of nursing, everything else can be shared. Be smart enough to share. Changing diapers, giving baths, rocking, and burping are all unisex. Sometimes the problem isn't that the husband won't help, but overly protective mothers have a hard time letting go long enough for their husband to get involved.

Today's husbands, and especially yours, seem to want to be involved with both mother and child. Don't resist his help, and don't be afraid to let go of responsibilities that can be shared.

Likewise, don't refuse help from others. It's possible to still be a good mother while letting someone else lend a helping hand.

The Psalmist tells us God doesn't sleep,

neither does He slumber. Only He can give nonstop care. People have to stop to rest their brain and renew their bodies. Don't be tempted to play God and think you can do everything.

Dedicated

*G*iving birth is much like a conversion experience. Seldom will you be as close to God or as thankful to His Spirit as when you receive the gift of a new life.

You know God is real.

You know God is good.

You know God is involved.

You know how much you need God.

Don't let that closeness fade away. Build on it. Your child will see your spirituality. True spirituality says that God is active in your lives and that you believe spiritual values are more important than temporal ones.

Every child deserves to see the Holy Spirit working in someone's life. Children will never have a better example than what they see in their parents.

Already you are talking about dedicating your baby. You feel that God gave you this child and you want to acknowledge that in a public way.

Your child will not be dedicated *to the church*, though that's important. You'll be dedicating your child *to the Lord*.

It's important for you as parents to be clear on what this really involves. What does it mean to you to be "dedicated to the Lord." Is it more than a ceremony? Are you asking for God's protection? Are you declaring your child belongs first to the Lord? Would you be happy to see the Lord bless others through the life of your child?

Too often dedication can be like "patriotism" or "love." The words are easy to say, but few people know what they really mean. Be convinced in your dedicating and in declaring what this act means to you and your child.

46

Preparing the Nursery

*S*ome third wedding anniversary! No flowers or candlelight dinner for you two. Not even an early movie at the discount theater. Instead, you spent your special day sanding and scraping paint in the nursery.

The best part of it all is that there's no place you would rather have been. That's because even moonlight cruises or sidewalk cafes can't compare with the sheer delight of getting ready for your new creation from inner space.

We laughed when we heard what you were doing. Not because we thought you

47

were silly or dumb, but because we knew. We knew your priorities were undergoing drastic changes. And we were happy for you.

There will still be time for romance, escapes, and watching sunsets on the beach. But for now, there are joys that no romantic getaway could ever match. You wouldn't trade your trips to Germany, California, or even Vermont for this greatest of all adventures.

Your nursery feels like love. It is neither overdone nor dull. It definitely has that "You're special" look and glow.

It's obvious the interior decorators of this room were an expectant mother and a satisfied father. Your love was evident as you collected each outfit, blanket, and piece of furniture.

Your friends contributed the baby's crib. The stroller came from Gerry's brothers and sisters. The dressing table your mother refinished was the same one your brother and sister used over twenty years ago.

New things are nice, but these things keep us connected. They reach back to

Gerry's family, your family, and the friends who care about you. Maybe it's just a mushy thought, but mushy thoughts are like glue and have a way of making us stick together.

A beautiful nursery is more than just a room where your baby will sleep and play. Preparing a nursery is part of a loving ritual. The preparation, the anticipation, the cleansing of your hearts. Each time you walk into the room, it's like breathing fresh air. Something is going to happen. Something so exciting and personal and miraculous that you will never be the same.

For now this room is a symbol of a gift too wonderful to comprehend.

Need a Baby-Sitter?

One of the toughest problems we had as parents of toddlers was getting baby-sitters. First, we couldn't afford one. Second, we couldn't find one. Third, we couldn't get one to come back.

It couldn't have been because we stayed out too late. Maybe it had something to do with the teeth marks on the sitter's ankles or the fires smoldering in the wastebaskets.

We'd like to volunteer to baby-sit from the very start. We want you to be able to count on us. Give us a baby and stock the fridge with your famous iced tea, and we'll come regularly.

We won't, however, be the kind of grandparents who will drop everything and run right over. We do have a life, a couple of hobbies, a bit of ministry, and some good friends we can't afford to dump without major cause.

But don't be bashful. Give us a call. If we can't come, we promise to say so. But we'll be there if we can. We place spending time with grandchildren right up there with hiking, fishing, and the Detroit Tigers.

We'll want to baby-sit at our house sometimes, too. I can teach our grandchild to watch *The Late Show*, eat ice cream at midnight, play chess, and enjoy country music (if you're lucky). There is nothing like a grandfather to corrupt an innocent tot—the donut shop, skull hunting, playing Nerts, hitting fly balls, watching for raccoons at night—every child needs this kind of exposure.

That's the price you pay for free baby-sitting, but what a deal!

We, therefore, take the grandparents' pledge:

We promise to spoil this child.

We promise to disregard half of all parental instructions.

We promise to mold this child to become exactly like Grandpa and Grandma.

Let us know how soon you'll be needing us.

The Perfect Child

*I*t's okay to expect to have a perfect child. Every parent does. Every parent should. There's never been a child exactly like this one, and there never will be again. Your child's DNA, fingerprints, and even his smell are totally unique.

Expect a perfect child. At least for a while. But never, ever, expect to be perfect parents. That's too idealistic to even dream about.

Just relax and get ready to mess up. If your baby starts crying, and you know all basic needs have been met, it's okay to give those lungs some exercise. Children are

53

better off if their demands are ignored from time to time.

What do you think you will do when your precious little one throws toys off the high-chair tray? Pick them up, of course. And if the toys go flying into space a second time? Try leaving them on the floor. Every child needs to learn the basic laws of physics. Toys that are thrown on the floor tend to remain on the floor. Consequently, children who want toys to play with will learn not to slam them to the linoleum.

Don't feel like a failure if sometime you lose your cool and shout back at your perfect child. Your child may scream at you daily and sometimes constantly, so if sometime you scream back, don't feel like a monster.

Walk away. Get a grip. Come back and smile again. Children love imperfect parents.

If your child can't read at age two or play the flute at age three, or if your offspring can't play chess or name the planets at age four, you can be proud. You must be neglecting all the right things.

What if your child colors outside the lines? Suppose sticky wrappers are left on your beautiful couch? How will you feel when you find the first crayon marks on the nursery wall? Or when your toddler makes a scene at the grocery store?

Those are all good signs of a perfect child with imperfect parents.

Every child needs two faithful, loving, caring parents who simply try to do what's right—parents who don't have the time, the energy, or the false pride to even aim for perfection.

Have a wonderfully imperfect time raising your perfect child.

Role Models

We can learn a lot from a good role model. I'm always impressed by people who are successful at what they do. I like to figure out how they do things and try to imitate them.

The people closest to us are usually our first examples. Which brings me to the sobering fact that, when it comes to motherhood, I have been your main role model. There are many things I wish I'd done differently when you kids were growing up.

1. I would have given your father more time and attention. I centered my life around my babies. We all would have been

better off if I'd allowed you kids to cry yourselves to sleep sometimes. Benign neglect
is okay.

2. I would have become a better cook.
Far too often dinners consisted of a quick
peanut butter sandwich, rather than a time
together that we could look forward to each
day. I'd follow the maxim: "Don't skimp on
food or lingerie."

3. I'd be brave enough to say no. Dad
was a pastor during the years you three
were born. As the pastor's wife, I felt it was
my duty to be at every service, prepare the
bulletin every Saturday night, teach Sun-
day school, take charge of nursery every
week, and handle phone calls any hour of
the day or night at the parsonage. I wish I'd
been more kind to myself and our family.

There are plenty of other things I know
now that I wish I'd known then. But those
are the big three. So, if you ever catch yourself doing things "because my mother did it
this way," remember your mom wishes she
would've done some of those things differently.

You have the opportunity now to weigh

what you've seen in other moms, and in me, and choose the way that is best for you.

Thankfully, there are some things I'd do over again:

Talk with and listen to my babies continuously.

Always be watchful for my babies' safety.

Remember that a mother knows her baby best; sometimes even professionals can be wrong.

The Day We Almost Lost You

*Y*ou were three months old on that cold December day we started our long drive east to visit your grandmother. We put you in a homemade car bed and wrapped you in blankets. We placed the bed in the backseat, and your mother sat beside you while I drove.

A freezing drizzle sprayed ever so lightly on the windshield as we drove off. We were cautious but not frightened. As we drove past Goshen, Indiana, the car suddenly went out of control on a slick curve. It slid

59

across the highway, through a barbed wire fence, bounced across a field, and rolled over on its side.

As I scrambled frantically out of the car, I asked your mother if she knew where you were. She said yes. But that's all she said.

In my panic I realized you'd been thrown out a window. I could see a small pink blanket wedged beneath the car. With my heart racing, I reached down to pick up what I thought was the crushed, silent body of my daughter.

I'll never forget the look on your face as I turned you over in my nervous hands. Your eyes were open as wide as saucers. Then you let out the loudest, most piercing cry in the history of babyhood. And it was the loveliest sound I'd ever heard.

A couple driving by stopped to help us. You cried all the way to the hospital and that was all we wanted you to do. Except for two tiny scratches on your face, the doctor couldn't find anything wrong with you.

The Lord was good to us. I don't know why other babies die and you were allowed to live. But we have always been grateful that God let us keep the one we love so much.

Hopefully nothing like this will happen to you. Intense drama isn't a key ingredient for a happy family. But don't be surprised when anxious moments come along.

Babies get sicker than we want them to be. They fall off things, get stuck in things, swallow things, and have closer calls than we want them to have. Some babies get burns, bites, blisters, and even lice.

It's all part of the process. Part of the challenge. Part of the irritation. Part of the unpredictability.

Part of growing up with the Lord.

Some days you might feel inadequate for the job. That's why we turn it over to Him. We do what we can. God adds His part, and we are grateful every day for the way things turn out.

What Does It Do?

 $\mathcal{Y}$ ears ago I gave a gift to a child. He looked at the small car, pulled at the doors, yanked at the wheels, and tugged at the trunk. Frustrated, he looked at me with a blank look and asked, "What does it do?"

The bewildered youngster was growing up thinking everything had to blip, buzz, twist, or flip. If it didn't, he thought the toy was as useless as a rock. He lived in the electronic world of joy sticks, computers, and videos.

Sophisticated toys are terrific. Every child should have their share of gadgets. (Even if each chip, ROM, and CD makes grandparents feel like cave people in an Internet world.)

But along the technological maze of life, do your child a favor and introduce life's simple pleasures.

Sandboxes don't need batteries.

Wild rabbits never rust.

Hunting four-leaf clovers doesn't require airline tickets.

A complicated life leaves children with a narrow view of the world. They start to believe that everything costs money, takes coupons, or appears first as a television ad.

It doesn't take $59.95 to find the North Star.

Roller-coaster rides don't compare with piggyback rides.

Video arcades dull next to prairie dog towns.

It would be a shame if a child couldn't bait a hook. What if all of a girl's dolls were models but none were babies? Imagine what it would be like if a child knew how to open presents but didn't know how to give any.

We promise to make it a point to introduce your child to the simple things God gave us. We'll give lessons on how to make bracelets out of flowers and the ancient art of opening seeds to paste on our noses or turn into nature's earrings.

We'll search with our grandchild to find the sweet smell of honeysuckle. Together we'll discover how it feels to touch the soft fur of the pussy willow. And on a cool spring morning we'll hunt for bird eggs and hope to see pecking chicks.

No doubt our grandchild will be a whiz with every device the new world has to offer. Maybe she'll even teach us to program our VCR before we go into the Home.

But for every gadget that depends on AC or DC, make sure your child also knows about a stream, a mountain, a cloud formation, and deer tracks through the forest. God's world is never more splendid than when it is at its simple best.

A White Sox Uniform

*H*alf the fun of preparing for your new arrival will be shopping in the Infant Department of your favorite stores. You'll find socks that resemble oversized thimbles, shirts too small for a doll, and bonnets that barely cover your fist. When one hasn't been around babies for a while, it is hard to remember how tiny their little bodies really are.

You've already received a great assortment of baby clothes in bright colors and creative designs. Your friends have had a great time sifting through the selections available.

Our favorite item is the little White Sox uniform. Gerry is particularly pleased at this token of his favorite team. He's such a proud father that he will be happy to see a rosy-cheeked girl or boy wearing those White Sox stripes.

Enjoy this time of preparation. Becoming parents for the first time is too exciting to miss out on any of its joys. You're getting a baby as well as all the unique equipment that comes with it. A spoon shaped like an airplane. Soft books to chew and read. Cuddly animals to hold and squeeze. They're all part of the small world of a bouncing beginner.

Drink it all in. Life passes too quickly into the next stage. Each stage is satisfying and challenging in its own right, but this first one has a charm different from any other.

When your baby arrives, play peek-a-boo behind the hooded towels. Wear funny things on your head to make the baby laugh. Rub that soft tummy till your baby beams and coos. Don't miss the special moments that come with this bundle of joy. These days are impossible to recapture, so make each one count.

Why Me, Lord?

*B*eing pregnant isn't a disease or a physical handicap. It didn't crash down on you like a brick from a second-story window. Unlike catastrophes, the victim (you!) actually tried to make it happen.

You read books, went to bed early, took a low stress job, prayed, and for all we know, ate mandrake roots like ancient Rachel. We doubt it was hard duty, and no doubt the two of you gave it your best.

Presto! By the grace of God, you passed the pharmaceutical test and received the happy news—you were pregnant!

This is all well and good. But about six

68

months into the pregnancy, about halfway between morning sickness and plumpness, this thought might cross your mind: Why me, Lord? That is to say, Why not my husband?

Let him get nauseated at the smell of fried chicken and pizza. Let him upchuck day and night. Let him gain forty pounds and have his ankles swell. Let him be short of breath and feel dizzy. Let him run to the bathroom every twenty-seven minutes.

Sometime during the nine months most moms think those thoughts. They want to know why the mister can't be the mom.

In saner moments you'll recognize these thoughts as feeling sorry for yourself. It's natural. It's normal. And it will pass.

There isn't a good answer to "Why me, Lord?" But most mothers don't really expect one. They are simply letting off some steam.

Eventually your thoughts will go back to gratitude and settle there. Mothers remember that God has answered their prayers. God has been faithful, loving, and close.

"Why?" is a philosophical question.

"What?" centers more on the practical. Most mothers become absorbed in what God has done and give up their questions of theory. Their unborn baby is reality. Look what the Lord has done!

Why didn't God deliver babies in coconuts? Couldn't they come drifting ashore, floating on lily pads? For some reason known only to Him, the Lord chose females to bear children and called them mothers. And He saw that it was good.

Self-pity can be transformed into satisfaction. Satisfaction will grow quickly into gratitude. And gratitude will give full rise in praise to God. We know it did for us.

Financial Concerns

Almost everybody worries about finances. Most families have problems making ends meet.

You've been self-sufficient for a long time. With limited help from your parents, you went through college and law school. Since your marriage, you and Gerry have purchased a home, furniture, and cars. There isn't much I could share about finances that you don't already know.

Long ago, you decided you would not work after your first child was born because you wanted to be a stay-at-home mom. I'm happy you have that option. In most cases, no one can give the same love and care as the baby's own mother.

Fortunately, you have good maternity insurance to help with delivery and hospital costs. There will be the additional costs of clothes, diapers or diaper service, doctor visits, formula, and baby food added to your budget after the baby is born.

Altering your lifestyle will be the first step in making your income fit the needs of your growing family. Never feel you have to keep up with others and have the latest in baby furniture and clothes. Accepting hand-me-downs and shopping at garage sales help stretch the budget. When friends ask what you need, be practical and let them know you don't plan to collect silver spoons.

Quite a few of the mothers in your circle of friends are employed. Some have chosen part-time work or a business they can pursue at home. Others have chosen full-time jobs. Some have grandparents to care for the children. When making choices about mothers working, couples need to total the costs of quality child care, wardrobe needs, taxes, convenience foods, hiring work done, and the costs of commuting before making a decision. They should ask themselves what is best for the baby and the family.

Jesus said, "So I tell you, don't worry about the food or drink you need to live, or about the clothes you need for your body. Life is more than food, and the body is more than clothes. Look at the birds in the air. They don't plant or harvest or store food in barns, but your heavenly Father feeds them. And you know that you are worth much more than the birds" (Matthew 6:25–27).

When you were born your dad was in his last year of seminary. He worked hard to keep up in classes and work a job, and God gave us all good health and much happiness.

The Modern Mixture

We hope our laughter doesn't bother you too much. It's just that the idea of taking breathing classes is more than we can handle. We had our babies thirty years ago, and somehow your mother knew instinctively that she should keep breathing.

Videotaping a birth isn't a concept that would have immediately come to our minds either. Though I must admit, those videos should certainly liven up boring family reunions!

Times have definitely changed and often for the best. Some things were better

74

the old way, but most things are better now. More babies get a better start, and more mothers come through childbirth in good health due to modern medicine and procedures. If the mother or baby develops problems, new medical procedures can head off a lot of complications.

At the same time, it's hard to beat the wisdom of an experienced mother and father. No book has ever walked the floor at 2:00 A.M. No scientific study can tell you what the sound of your baby's cry means. No pamphlet has held its own newborn and felt her warm breath or watched her smile for the first time.

We are willing to admit it. We may not think we're getting old, but we can't be too far away. Our memories take us back to a time when things were real. It wasn't necessarily a better era, but it certainly was different.

We can remember when
stadium grass was natural
hamburgers were made of meat
telemarketers never called during
dinner

teachers were always right

people got married and then had babies

pregnant women were given seats on
the bus

and diapers were real.

Frankly, we love change. Not all changes are good, but in many ways parents are better off today than they used to be. Many are better educated, better prepared, and very loving people.

Modern technology and experienced parents don't always agree. And who's to know which is right? You seem smart enough to listen to both and then to pick and choose. May God give us the grace to stay open-minded.

You'll have to excuse us if we chuckle at some of the things we hear. Sometimes we're doing our best not to laugh aloud. We've seen fads come and go, and fortunately the really good ones have remained to help babies and mothers everywhere.

Go for it. Be tomorrow's mother. You can never go back to the future.

If you want advice, we'll simply tell you what worked and what didn't work for us. We want you to do things the best way for you and your baby.

Support Groups

J read in a recent article that a support group is vital to an individual's good health.

Family is a wonderful support group. Your dad and I won't schedule any trips during the month of June so we can be available to help you. Thank you for inviting me to stay with you for a few days after the baby is born. I'm flattered to be asked to help, though you and Gerry are excellently prepared parents-to-be and could manage superbly alone.

I can prepare meals, do laundry, and whatever else will be of help to you. Then

I'll go out in the evenings so you three can spend time together.

We never want to interfere after the baby arrives, and we'll do our best to stay away except when you want us. Perhaps when the baby is old enough to be left with baby-sitters, we can come down once a week and give you an afternoon out. Maybe we can take over for an evening now and then so you and Gerry can date. We certainly want you to call us if you are ever sick or overwhelmed and need help.

My goal is to be a good neighbor and know when to come over and when to stay off your doorstep.

Another support group is your church. You have many friends there who care about you and will be ready to help. Your baby is fortunate because your church is an important part of your family life. Your child will have fun growing up with Claire, Hannah, Ben, Kaitlin, and all the other children.

It looks like you have at least two good support groups already in place.

Your Attitude Is Showing

*C*hildren worry about being poor if their parents worry about it. They think they have grouchy neighbors if Mom and Dad complain about the people next door. Children believe the world is falling apart if their parents are pessimistic, continuously predicting doom.

Attitudes are contagious. That's why we like the atmosphere at your home. The two of you aren't bouncing around from crisis to crisis. You don't act like there is a threat lurking behind every door.

Babies pick up anxiety from their parents like a new vacuum cleaner inhales dust. They are just as quick to gather up good qualities such as security, peace, and joy. Babies love to see happy parents. The smile on a baby's face doesn't really come from gas. An infant grins from ear to ear because she wants to look like Mom and Dad.

So what are parents to do? Should they put on smiley faces, gush like cosmetic salespeople, and sing clever jingles? Pretending is a waste of time. Children can see through a mask. They feel vibrations. Babies pick up on electrical static in the room. Children with miserable parents sometimes experience rashes and hair loss.

Pretending won't cut it. Babies soon learn if there are turbulent currents beneath the tranquil sea.

Parents at peace is high on the list of great gifts to give your children. Not that they don't squabble or express their discontent. Babies aren't devastated by the occasional storm that blows through the house. What hurts is the chill they feel as their parents' temperature stays cold or the sweat they feel as the emotional climate remains too heated.

Keep in close touch. Stay close to each other. Stay close to the Lord. Let the cheerful optimism of your faith run deep into your hearts and souls. As you pray and read from God's Word, your baby will sense your peace and feel secure. When we read portions of *Little Visits With God* at mealtimes, it drew our family closer and taught what is good and right.

Your baby will know the genuineness of your spirituality from the start. Someone said spirituality is so important that everyone should have it even if they have to fake it. But children know we can't fake it. Only manipulative, pretentious adults believe in the facade of spirituality.

Your baby will someday thank God for good parents (say, when she's around 25 years old). Your child will realize where her strengths and stability come from.

And your child will be grateful.

Naturally Noisy

*H*ow can a mother tell if she has a "good" baby? Far too many parents have only one gauge for goodness. They have but one criteria, one goal. They believe their lives have been blessed if they have a quiet baby.

Watch an average parent. The minute the child starts to make a fuss, parents go to almost any extreme to hush the little creature.

Their first impulse is to grab a plug and stick it in the child's mouth. A bottle, a pacifier, a finger, a toy—anything that will fit.

It's almost as if the baby has no right to

make noise. Why is that? Mom, Dad, brother, sister, and Bruno the dog are all allowed to talk, laugh, sing, bark, and even cry. But let baby express himself and everyone pounces on the kid.

Parents don't want anyone to think their child is "bad." And the surest sign of infant delinquency is their perchance to use verbal expression. Any attempt to complain or wail is met with instant oral discipline.

Actually there's little wrong with letting baby cry. Is baby dry? Is baby well-fed? Is baby still crying? Then a good crying session may simply be ignored.

This might sound like radical parenting, but sometimes babies learn by crying. They train adults through the wailing method. Adults can be taught to jump up, rush in, pick up the child, rock, feed, entertain, and produce almost anything.

Babies don't train us with whips and chairs. They use neither carrots nor sticks to motivate grown-ups. Children don't promise bonuses, pay raises, or retirement perks. All they need to do is play the crying game with a masterful touch and adults quickly respond.

And don't think baby is too innocent to manipulate adults. They have on-the-job training and within a few weeks may be heavily into finger-wrapping—the art of wrapping adults around their tiny little digits.

However, when it comes to grand-parents, none of the regular rules apply. If Grandma and Grandpa respond to every whimper, whine, and sniffle, they are just fulfilling their duty. They're exempt from al-most all laws of child discipline. But par-ents have to act more responsibly.

Not all babies are noisy. Some will sim-ply ignore their parents and pretty much entertain themselves. The ones that need to be watched are the pouters and blubberers. They're testing the parental waters to check the temperature. Parents will have to de-cide if they want to encourage that type of noise or help control it.

Mood Music

Why do some stores start playing Christmas music the morning after Halloween? Why do elevators pipe in soothing sounds for their occupants? Why is the music at a ball park upbeat, loud, and energetic?

Music has always helped create atmosphere. Even background music tells us everything's cool or that things are hopping. Children don't have to take music lessons to understand that sounds seriously affect our moods.

That's why children like to hear their parents sing to them. To them the sound is soothing. It's personal. It's reassuring. Babies don't grade friends and relatives on tonal quality. They give points for sincerity, love, and intentions. Those aren't the same qualities we need to join the choir, but you can't wear your bathrobe in the tenor section, either.

Some of our earliest memories are of our mothers singing to us as we rocked on the porch. Perfectly content, we played with her necklace while her songs, hymns, or humming assured us that everything was under control.

Music is a medicine sent like a rare herb to help cure our ills and maintain good health. The right music at the right time does the heart, soul, and mind good. There's some possibility that the wrong music could also drive us to distraction.

Look for cassettes and CDs with your infant in mind. Which kinds of music say everything's calm and running on an even keel? Which tunes suggest that your lives are filled with rejoicing and anticipation?

Your child might not remember one song from the early childhood years, but that isn't the goal. The intention is to set the mood for each day—a tune communicating that the present is good, and that we'll be happy to let God handle the future.

Breast-Feeding

J was one of those fortunate mothers who was able to breast-feed her children. It's one of the great experiences God gives to many mothers.

I'm glad you're convinced that breast-feeding is normally best for a baby. It's the perfect food with the perfect delivery system.

Nursing is also good for the mother. It helps speed the shrinking of the uterus back to its pre-pregnant size. Breast-feeding brings you and baby together, skin to skin, to share love and closeness. It's the healthiest, safest, most convenient, and most economical way to feed your baby.

At the hospital a nurse will put the new-born to your breast within minutes of the birth. At first the baby will get tiny amounts of colostrum. This provides your baby with enough nourishment for now and important antibodies his or her own body can't yet produce, while helping to empty the digestive system of excess mucus and the bowels of meconium. By the third or fourth day your breasts will begin to feel full, indicating that your milk has come in.

Your hospital provides rooming-in so you can have the baby with you. Feel free to ask visitors to leave when it's time to feed your baby. The goal is to provide an environment where you feel calm and relaxed. Find a comfortable position and patiently help the baby latch onto the entire nipple. A nurse can assist you if you have problems.

Some hospitals have lactation specialists or volunteers from the La Leche League to provide assistance.

The first couple of weeks may be awkward as the milk supply adjusts to your baby's need. Sometimes you will wonder if baby is getting enough to eat, and other times your milk will spill over between nursings. Your breasts may get sore, or your nipples may crack, or your breasts may become engorged (too full). All this is natural and normal. Don't give up. A good book will give many suggestions to alleviate these problems. Soon you and the baby will adjust to each other, and your body will know how much milk to produce.

During the months that you breast-feed, eating a well-balanced diet and drinking lots of liquids are very important.

If for any reason you find breast-feeding is not working for you, you can always begin bottle-feeding. Many healthy babies are bottle-fed.

You have made a good choice. Your baby will have a great start in life, and you'll discover another of the rich joys of motherhood.

Birth Order

*I*t has become popular to study birth order and how it affects each child. Child number three is supposed to have a certain type of personality. Number one is another variety, and child number two is a baloney sandwich.

At the risk of sounding anti-intellectual, let us deliver this warning: don't simply accept this system and expect your child to slide into a predetermined behavior pattern.

To a great extent your child will decide what he wants to be and he will make those decisions early. If we read the literature and then begin to anticipate how each child will behave, we'll soon see that exact behavior coming through.

Back off. Let the baby become herself. Whether she's caring or headstrong, driving or relaxed, let the baby work that out. Pleasing, compliant, independent or defiant, the child will have to wrestle with those traits inside her own heart and soul.

We promise we won't sit around saying goofy things like, "The baby is trying to make everyone happy. Isn't that just like a first child?" or "The baby won't let go of Grandpa's expensive watch. Second children do that, you know."

Our professional friends tell us we're foolish to ignore the birth order concept. Maybe. But we can study people to death. We can make the mistake of trying to put everyone into designated pigeonholes.

The creativity of God is far more diverse than we might think. Babies are free to construct their own personalities out of the erector set of life. If a firstborn wants to be demanding, rebellious, perfectionist, curious, and jovial all at once, she certainly has

93

the freedom to do it all.

Children are like packages. They open up at their own rates and reveal their contents as they choose. They weren't produced on assembly lines. They'll develop and grow in response to the stimuli they find around them. But the responses will be their own.

We're glad that no one told us what you were supposed to be like. It was too much fun watching you become your own person.

🐑

Memories of a Miscarriage

$\mathcal{N}$ot everything goes smoothly. Much of life is dedicated to problem-solving. What do we do when our heart is broken? How do we get back into the race after we have the wind knocked out of us?

We remember well what happened a year ago. We didn't know anything had gone wrong until Pastor Steve called. He wanted to know the name of the hospital where you were in Minneapolis. After being up all night and returning from the hospital, you called the church just before the morning service and then went to sleep, deciding to call us afterward with the sad news. A smart move on your part, but one event accidently jumped ahead of the other.

When the two of you got back to Lincoln, we could see devastation written all over your faces. It wasn't that a dream had been lost. It wasn't that a mere detour had been placed in your journey. The truth was written on your tear-stained faces. A life had been lost. Part of your flesh and blood was gone.

Thanks for telling us what not to say. We were ready with dumb cliches. You weren't looking for explanations or excuses. You'd lost your child. The child you'll never know or get to play with in this world. The toes you won't get to count and the cheeks you'll never kiss are gone.

You didn't care what the court says or what the hospital says or even what the minister says. One fact will never change: you lost your child.

We remember you saying you would always wonder what the baby's personality would have been like. We wonder, too.

We've learned how much it hurts to see people you love in pain.

We rejoice that the two of you had the courage to try again. And soon you'll reap the reward of your hope.

It's miraculous that God gives us the will to bounce back. That's one of His better gifts.

Life means more to us when we remember how fragile it is. We are all tough, resilient, and resourceful. And yet all of us hang by a thread.

We pay tribute to the child of your miscarriage.

Don't Forget the King

*I*t happens. We've seen it happen to
hundreds of couples. It happened to
us.

Immediately after the birth, a baby becomes the main attraction. It's only natural.
The little doll will be cute as a bug, helpless, and irresistible. Relatives and friends
will come from far and wide just to see this
new creation.

As the center of your universe shifts to
feeding, rocking, and diaper changes,
someone might feel left out. Yesterday your
husband felt like the king; today he's been
demoted to butler.

That won't hurt a husband for a little while, but the problem with too many marriages is that the wife forgets he exists. It can be literally fifteen years in some marriages before he gets even close to the limelight again.

Don't let yourselves become a child-centered family. No one wants to be displaced. It doesn't feel good to be taken for granted. It's humiliating for a husband to have to raise his hand and say, "Hey, do you remember me?"

Too many couples have lost the romance in their relationship and settled into a dull routine. They argue over utility bills and are busy trying to scrape up enough money for children's athletic shoes.

No one dare neglect a child, but couples can't afford to neglect each other either.

Plan time for each other. Do the things that are special to the two of you. They don't have to be expensive, but they do need to be personal and caring.

Before the baby arrived, you were a couple, and by the grace of God, you will one day be a couple again. Do whatever it takes

99

along the way to keep the bonds tight and close between you.

It works differently for everyone, but it needs to work. Married love is too great a treasure to simply misplace and be unable to find when the nest is empty.

Time to Play

Caring for a new baby is a lot of work. You'll have lists of duties, chores, responsibilities, and errands you never knew existed. You might feel like you can't ever accomplish enough in one day, and wonder how you'll know if you're being a good parent.

Here's a good gauge to use in measuring your success:

Any day in which you spend time playing with your baby is a day put to good use. Days when all your lists keep you from playtime need improvement.

Aren't other things as important as playing? Yes. Are there other things *more* important than playing? Probably not.

If we could ask a fox to tell us the keys to good parenting, it would respond with "playfulness." Father and Mother fox don't think a baby is ready to shake out of the den until it has played hard and long with its parents.

Playfulness is the serious work of human parents, too. Children need to know the lighter side. They need to hear caring adults chuckle, giggle, and roar with laughter. Children who grow up with stern parents aren't sure it's all right to laugh and play. Parents who provide fun times of laughter enable their babies to enjoy the years and decades to come.

Children naturally want to smile. They learn how by seeing smiles on their mother's and father's faces. They see wide grins and sparkling eyes, and they want to smile too.

Roll on the floor with your baby. Let him ride on your back and hold on with a tight, tiny grip. Lie on your back and let her climb up and over your stomach. Babies love tussling and tugging with the people who love them.

On those days when the bathroom needs cleaning and the living room is a dusty disaster; when the kitchen counter isn't cleared off and the beds haven't been made; when you feel behind and plenty guilty, take ten extra minutes to play with your baby. Let the housework go, the grass grow, and the windows wait. Take ten more minutes to play with one of God's greatest gifts.

Then you'll know you have your priorities in order.

Back Rubs

One of the best things you can do for your baby is touch him. That sounds too obvious for some parents, while other parents draw back and avoid contact with their child.

Some parents are uncomfortable with touching. Others are unaccustomed to physical contact. Sometimes parents assume they touch their baby more than they actually do.

Babies who are touched often, slowly and lovingly, tend to feel secure and accepted. They are more calm and tend to live life at a peaceful pace.

On a regular basis, lay your baby down and slowly massage the little body from head to toe. Rub her tiny feet. Play with his toes. Knead those chubby legs. Slowly spread oil over the baby's small chest and bottom. Put the infant on your shoulder and pat his back. Walk and rock and sing together.

Take your time. Don't be quick or rough. Be firm. Be gentle. Talk to your new-born in a reassuring voice. Hum now and then. Having a daily routine like this will provide a strong sense of security for your baby.

Babies catch on quickly. They know when they are in a safe place. Make sure Dad puts in equal time. The touch and presence of each parent adds to a child's stability.

Some children grow up unfamiliar with a loving, family touch. In later years, they may go looking for its imitation or else re-main afraid of any kind of touch.

One of life's greatest thrills is to walk along with a tottering toddler reaching up to hold your index finger. They want you, they need you, and they will follow you almost anywhere.

The physical touch of a baby born of your own womb, flesh of your flesh, is one of the greatest rushes any of us will experience in this world. Give regular messages—skin to skin. Your baby may not remember it, but the benefits will never be forgotten.

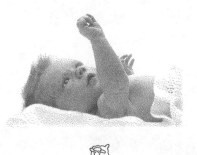

Be Sure to Baby-Proof

$\mathcal{W}$here did Mary go?

It was one of those sudden rushes of fear that comes over a parent who senses something is wrong.

We ran out of the room in search of our little crawling creature. You couldn't have gone far. You couldn't even walk. Turning toward the hall we looked up the staircase and there you sat. You had somehow wriggled and struggled up each step and perched yourself near the top.

Proudly you sat there in your frilly pink dress, a huge grin plastered across your satisfied face. Then you began to bounce gently back and forth like an otter on a rock.

"Don't move!" we pleaded.

"Stay still!" we begged.

Two panic-stricken parents started cautiously up the steps. We had visions of Humpty Dumpty, for we were certain that at any moment you would totter forward, lose your balance, and come tumbling headlong toward us.

Fortunately, you didn't come crashing down, and we didn't need all the king's horses and men to put you back together again. But it was a good lesson in infant safety.

We'll think "safety" as our grandchild gets ready to make a grand entrance.

Are liquids and chemicals removed from beneath the sink?

Are the stairs child-proof?

Is the crib padded and are the rungs and mattress safe?

Is the car seat the safest kind?

Is the paint in the nursery free of toxins?

Are electronic devices well secured?

Is the toilet seat down?
Are boxes out of reach?
Where is the sewing basket?
Are there plants the baby could eat?
Do tablecloths or cords hang down?
Are cabinet doors secure?

Contact your county extension agent for safety tips. Walk through the house over and over again and repeat these three words:

Crawl
Grab
Swallow

And when you come to our house, please remind us of anything we've overlooked.

Expect a scare now and then. Normally babies squeak through with a minimum of bruises. Parents, however, suffer quite a few panic attacks.

Try to remember. If you hear the baby cooing contentedly in the distance, run and check the top of the stairs.

The Self-Esteem Thing

On one hand, too much has been made of this self-esteem thing. On the other hand, we haven't yet put enough emphasis on it. The problem of poor self-esteem is real but maybe not as all-consuming as some would have us think.

As usual, we'll share our thoughts on achieving the perfect balance.

Parents help contribute to a child's sense of self-worth. But parents are not the sole controlling factor. You can help your child feel confident and worthwhile up to a point. However, the child must eventually make some decisions of his own.

Children will sift through several re-
sources:

their environment
genetics
personal choices
and their parental input.

From those four, and possibly other
sources we don't understand, children will
grapple with their own self-esteem. Parents
have some effect on the outcome, but nothing near being the controlling factor.

Every person must decide how he will
evaluate himself. We all process data differently and come to our own conclusions.

This doesn't mean parents are without
influence. Far from it. You have the opportunity to:

Show your child your self-confidence
Praise your child
Let your child go, but not too far
Live an example of optimism
Speak of your faith and of your fears.

Having done that, be content. Never,
never, never take the responsibility for how
your children feel about themselves. Parents contribute; they do not control.

Too often parents program their child for confidence, only to see the opposite occur.

You won't be the ideal parents. Your baby won't be perfect. But what a terrific family you'll all make.

Ignore the Ads

*H*ave you checked out the television ad where the woman looks so earnest and says that the dream of every mother is to have her child become a doctor? Try again. What is this ad trying to do? It wants to sell every parent a certain set of books. If the ad can manipulate a mother's dreams so she will buy the books, the merchandiser is happy.

Parents are naturally caring, protective, and idealistic. They are also prone to guilt. Some advertisers play on sensitive parents' loving instincts. Watch out. Don't fall for every educational tool and health aid that appears in magazines, on television, or radio.

We used to worry about perfect shoes. We bought expensive, hard-sole shoes for you while you were still flat on your back in the cradle. Shoes you'd never even stand in, let alone take your first steps.

But we believed the sales pitch. Babies' first shoes should help form their little feet. We bought the pitch and the shoes.

As highly susceptible parents, we could have purchased all kinds of things. Alphabet toys, educational tapes, scientific picture books. All designed to jump-start baby and propel her into the educational future.

We bought our share of dumb things. If we'd listened to all of the ads, we would have gone broke and turned you into a knowledge-spouting machine.

Not that we were opposed to education. But this question kept haunting us. If our child becomes a three-year-old nuclear physicist, when will she have time to be a child? Will she have to regroup at age thirty-five and learn how to play, color, and pull the cat's tail? Will she have to quit her job at the computer headquarters so she'll be able to build castles in a backyard sandbox?

Ads are all right and books are great for any child. But don't let the nation's merchandisers tell you what's best for your baby's future. The temptation is to let the youngster's childhood be wrestled away.

Some of the greatest thinkers, creators, inventors, and entrepreneurs of our country were considered dull when they were children. They took their time and blossomed when the time was right for them.

Any educational toy being pitched by a salesman should give you cause for pause. Their first concern might not be your child's education and development. Their major interest could be paying for the education of their own children.

Eating Out

We enjoy looking under restaurant tables after a family with three or four children leaves. The floor looks like a birdcage. It's covered with crumbs, napkins, spoons, paper cups, ribbons, and toys. Waiters and busboys rush in like street cleaners, brooms flying, dustpans rolling, and vacuum cleaners roaring across the carpet.

What a wonderful sight. Another family has enjoyed a festival of fries, milk shakes, burgers, and ice cream. They've completed the modern ritual of eating out.

Most parents feel awkward the first

time they take their child to a restaurant or a fast food pit. They're afraid their kids will act up, throw a fit, and make a scene. And, of course, they will. But it has to happen, unless you leave your child at home until age twelve.

As parents who have been totally embarrassed by their own children in more than one eating place, and as adults who have watched thousands of other children, we have a few observations. This isn't advice, so you can follow what you want. These aren't commands, so don't feel compelled to do the exact opposite. They are only observations to note and consider.

- No food throwing—other people don't appreciate flying oatmeal.
- No screaming—a little crying is all right, but remove wailers.
- Don't out-yell them—it's obnoxious when adults keep raising their voices.
- Don't even think about making a quick diaper change at the table.
- Have the children remain seated— running, crawling, scooting, and playing tag in the aisles give the other

customers indigestion.

- Don't smack, spank, or shake—take the child outside, settle the issue, and bring the tamed little angel back.
- Teach them to keep food in their mouths—only in an absolute emergency may a child spit out food.
- Try to keep it to two children per adult—usually children deserve the attention of at least one half of an adult.

As time goes by you'll make up your own list of guidelines. But be sure and take children with you when you can. They deserve the fun and excitement.

Bon appetit.

Am I Still Sexy?

*I*t's hard to feel attractive when you're carrying extra pounds and most of it sticks out in front like a watermelon. Mirrors aren't exactly flattering—if you can manage to get all of yourself inside one mirror frame, that is.

Getting used to your changing figure is an adjustment. It's tough to look at magazines and see lithe ladies tucked securely into wispy bathing suits.

But one step at a time. You certainly were sexy. Your present condition is proof of that. And your shape will be appealing again.

Most good gifts have a price. It'll cost you plenty to get this bundle of sunshine. Your husband will also pay for the experience, but his payments will be different. Don't fight reality. You have to make room for your new addition, and God made your body so it would provide flexible housing.

For now, be content to be pregnant. Take satisfaction in your newfound shape. Don't try to stay slim, look curvy, and be nine months pregnant at the same time. Mixed goals only lead to frustration and even despair.

The King James Bible says Mary the mother of Jesus was "great with child." Now you can understand firsthand that great was a euphemism for "really big."

We all make the mistake of fighting the wrong battles at the wrong times. For now your figure is perfect. It needs to curve exactly the way it does. After the delivery you can relax and watch your body realign itself and seek out a different direction.

The answer is a definite yes. You will look sexy again, and your husband will be after you like a bee on a flower.

Three Weeks!

That's what the lady said. She was showing us her new baby when the subject turned to her mother.

"She was a big help," the lady explained. "My mom moved in with us for three weeks and ran the household."

We looked for the same glimmer of joy in her husband's eyes, but it simply wasn't there. He looked more like he'd spent his vacation at the dentist.

Don't worry. We won't be moving in. A few days to help you get started and that's it. The rest of the time you'll have to give us a call.

You might appreciate a few home-cooked meals. A quick run with the vacuum might even come in handy. But no one's coming to camp at your house.

Even modern mothers admit they would like a steady hand the first couple of days. The baby's first bath can be a tad tricky. You also might be befuddled over those early crying spells. Every baby has its own system of signals. You might need a lesson or two on how to read the clues.

But you and Gerry will want plenty of time alone. We have a great deal of respect for that need. We promise to tiptoe around, up and down, out the front door.

Speak up and let us know how we can help. We aren't always great at guessing. Three weeks *might* be a bit much, but who knows, maybe we'll start to feel right at home!

🐑

Will I Get Lonely?

The life of a stay-at-home mother can become terribly lonely. All of your energies, interests, and communication are centered around the baby. The baby doesn't speak your language, read books, or understand the latest television talk show. Infants don't care if politicians lie, the mail runs two days late, or if the Chinese food has too much sodium in its sauce.

But that's not to fault your child. Babies understand what's really important in life. They are extremely concerned about food, drink, dry diapers, pacifiers, and physical contact. How can people go wrong if they concentrate on those essentials?

But, yes, babies are limited companions. They don't hold up their end of conversations, and their aerobic exercises consist mostly of fist clenching, leg kicking, and a regular routine of vocal straining.

If you want to keep your sanity, call a few friends and get out of the house from time to time. Any mother who speaks "goo-goo," "koochie-coo" and "baby-waby" all day is bound to lose thirty points from her previous IQ. Baby talk, nose rubbing, and drying bottoms with a hair dryer is too narrow a challenge, even for the most dedicated mother.

Go to the park by yourself (don't forget to have someone watch the baby). Read an outrageous book. Join a support group for novice mothers. Attend a Bible study and take advantage of your sister's offer to baby-sit.

Don't let yourself become the Lone Ranger. Let your husband help. He's very capable. Let grandparents take their turn. We will love every minute of it. Don't be the reticent hermit who refuses any form of assistance. Many mothers who reject everyone's help later look back and regret it.

Some mothers feel that the greatest gift they give their child is their *undivided* attention. The fact is that some mothers would help everyone by giving their child their *divided* attention. No mother should neglect her baby. Rather, every mother should let others share the load while Mom escapes from the cage every now and then.

The happy mother still speaks to adults about adult things.

The happy mother takes time every day for herself.

The happy mother accepts help.

The happy mother reads the newspaper.

The happy mother doesn't discourage her husband from helping.

The happy mother goes to the library and picks over the new books.

The happy mother sits with friends and talks about anything she wants to.

Happy mothers refuse to lock themselves in with their babies all day and all night.

Be a happy mom.

A Wednesday Matinee

*L*et's plan on it. The month of June will be hot, you'll be carrying an extra thirty-five pounds around, and the baby will probably be late. Let's pick out an air-conditioned theater some afternoon and go to a movie. How about seeing a comedy with a silly plot and plenty of funny lines? You won't want anything too dramatic.

Take my advice and expect the baby to be late. First babies often seem timid and like to hang out in a secure womb for a little extra rest.

Doctors set dates, but even they know mothers have to hang loose. How much difference do a couple of weeks make to a little snuggle bunny with his whole life ahead?

Don't become too impatient after you've tired of reading books and doing needlepoint. You don't remember, but you took your time and refused to make your grand appearance until two full weeks after we expected you.

Your friends might begin to bug you. They want to know every four hours if you've gone to the hospital. You'll get tired of being asked, but remember they love you and are anxious to share in your happiness.

You probably won't be able to sleep well at night, so take naps during the day. Keep up your strength for the big event. Your baby might like it when you take walks, as the motion rocks her to sleep.

Extra time on your hands gives you the opportunity to check in with the Lord. Time belongs to Him. Your times are in His hands. Tell Him again how you feel about this special present and about your hopes and dreams for your baby. The clock might still crawl along, but time will be well spent getting your spiritual bearings.

See you at the movies.

The Big Night

The big night could mean anything, so keep your cool. Your baby might come quickly or take his time. It could mean rushing to the hospital in the middle of the night, or the big night could take place during the day.

Babies can be born anywhere. We wish someone had told us that. Hospitals may be best, but sometimes you have to improvise.

You came almost exactly like the book said you would. Your mother counted the hours, timed the pains, and called the doctor at precisely the right hour. We dashed off to the hospital. Your mother checked in and sent me home to eat breakfast.

No sooner had I returned to the waiting room than a nurse came up and said, "Mr. Coleman, would you like to meet your new daughter?" You were wiggling and crying.

Your arrival was a total joy. And it still is.

Jim's grand entrance was a tad more unusual. The contractions closed in at 2:00 A.M. We dropped you off at a friend's house and headed down the highway. Just as we drove onto the Ford Freeway, your mother said, "I never had this much pain with Mary."

Jim began to make his move.

Your mother remained calm and I tried to get arrested. I beeped the horn, turned the headlights on and off, and annihilated the speed limit. But police were nowhere to be found.

When Jim howled his first cry we felt great relief. His lungs were in great shape. He liked being born in a car.

Spotting an all-night factory, we stopped to use the phone. I quickly called an emergency number and the attendant said, "Is the baby crying?"

"Yes, sir."

"Your best bet is to get back in the car and drive to the hospital."

We'll never forget the look on the nurse's face in the emergency room.

"I have a newborn in the car," I told her.

"Where's the mother?"

"Oh, she's in the car, too."

All havoc broke loose and medical personnel ran in every direction.

We can only tell you what the big night might bring.

Baby-Time

verything is under control. Your overnight bag is packed for the hospital. Gerry has exact instructions about what to do. You've measured the distance to the emergency room and know precisely how long the trip will take.

The "due date" has been written on the calendar for months. Everyone's activities have been planned around this magical time.

But don't be surprised or disappointed if that date comes and goes without a birthday. Your baby will choose his own time to make the grand entry. She might get impatient and hurry the system by a few weeks. On the other hand, baby might decide to lean back, practice kicking a little more, and gain another pound or two before arriving on the scene.

Babies have their own schedule, and the sooner Mom accepts that fact, the better it is for everyone. Babies don't read the charts and don't much care when the doctor wants to golf. Left alone, babies determine their own timetables.

This gives you a chance to get used to your new time zone. For years to come you'll be on "baby-time."

Babies decide when they want to cry. They sleep when they're in the mood, no matter what mood Mom is in. If Mom says it's lunch time, baby might not agree. Who do you think is going to win that argument?

Slowly you can start to share time zones with the baby, but at first parents are at the infant's mercy. That's especially hard on independent parents who are used to calling their own shots.

A hundred times you'll say to your toddler, "Now let's hurry and eat so we can go."

133

Like most parents, you will learn that schedules, clocks, planning, promptness, and routines are not as powerful as you thought. People are more important than programs. Holding a baby takes priority over getting to the ball game on time.

If the baby takes her time to arrive, don't get upset. She may be sending a message. The message is "Make room for me. I have a mind of my own."

A "late" birth may be one of God's kindest gifts. He wants to give you time to adjust to a new way of thinking. Baby-time is just as important as Eastern Time, parent-time, or hurry-time.

Baby-time reminds us that other people matter, too. Sometimes we need to slow down and wait for the people we love.

Childbirth

*Y*our baby is due to arrive any day now, and you're no doubt a little scared. Apprehension is normal, especially with the first baby.

Your choice of natural childbirth sounds very safe, using walking, exercising, and proper breathing to help speed and ease the pain of delivery. You're in good hands with the midwife/doctor team. They view childbirth as a body's natural process and feel medical personnel are present just to help things along.

You worked hard to find the right hospital, a fine one where rooming-in is encouraged. Gerry and your baby even get their own beds, right in your room! What a secure environment for your new family. Gerry will assist the nurse in giving the baby's first bath and help care for the baby while you are in the hospital. Don't hesitate to call the nurses, though. You'll have been through a lot, and deserve some pampering. Let them know what you need.

Birth is imminent. You and the baby are healthy and strong. You're ready to do anything to get this baby out! It sounds like everything is in order for the big event.

Our prayers are with you, Mary. I hope you'll be comforted by knowing God is present with you. He created the marvelous plan of birth and your child is loved by Him.

Soon. It sounds nice. We can't promise any more than that. But soon you and Gerry will share the joy of holding your baby.

Wonderfully Made

*H*e isn't so tiny after all! All of his nine pounds, ten ounces look healthy, happy, and confident. It's a fantastic experience to see our grandson. It's sheer delight to hold the little guy for the first time. What a bundle of happiness God has passed on to us.

Aren't babies supposed to be wrinkled and little? He's so long and so perfectly proportioned. We'll have to take his newborn-size clothes back to the store and exchange them for something in the men's department!

The hospital staff seems to think he

wasn't very late after all. They say that's one of the reasons why he isn't wrinkled.

In some mysterious, poetic way God has been knitting your son together for these nine months, and what a fine job He did. The small fingers, cute little ears, and squinty eyes are a marvel to see. All of us are tremendously thankful to a God who gives indescribable gifts like this.

The author of Psalm 139 said it for us:
"For you created my inmost being;
you knit me together in my mother's
womb.
I praise you because I am fearfully and
wonderfully made;
Your works are wonderful,
I know that full well." (vss. 13, 14)

We've seen oceans and we've hiked up mountain trails. We've stood beside thousand-foot waterfalls and looked out over rippling plains. We've even seen tornadoes and hurricanes. But none of these compare in pure majesty and wonder to the sight of this newborn baby. God can be seen in the vastness of creation, but to be really appreciated, His smaller works speak best. We marvel at the intricate touches, the fine points and the finished product, of a loving Master who cares so much for His creations.

The big day has come! We've met a new person and we love him dearly. God has filled our hearts with His gift.

Thank you, mother and child, for coming our way.

A New Name

*Y*ou picked the perfect name. You knew it could be done. You knew it needed to be done. And you did it.

Nolan Michael. The angels themselves couldn't have made a better selection. It has just the right combination of character, strength, and tenderness. He's off to a great start with a well-balanced name like that.

You and Gerry labored over names as though you were examining shiny rocks in an ancient river bed. Hundreds of names were held up, one at a time, and examined in the light.

You held each name in your hand and

checked its weight. Some were too big, while others were too light. Then came the perfect one. It felt right. No amount of logic can explain the decision. Based not so much on reason as it was on conviction, this name fit your baby even though you had yet to meet him. Only a parent can know for sure.

Names aren't simply titles or tags. They aren't so much a designation as they are a canonization. Your hopes, dreams, and joys are expressed in a handful of consonants and vowels. To the best of your ability the name projects who you hope this person will become.

The name Nolan Michael represents what moms and dads everywhere feel. Their love has turned into a human being, and this being is worth naming, keeping, loving, and protecting. The name Nolan will always call a precious face to your mind as you remember the gift God has given you.

Nesting Places

*Y*ou'll find birds nesting in trees and ostrich nests on flat ground. Penguins like to nest on their father's feet.

Babies have their favorite places to nest, too. Nolan will soon pick out a few places where he especially enjoys nestling and snuggling.

Don't be surprised if these are some of his best nests:

- *Babies love to lie on a grandfather's chest.*

If Grandpa will stretch out on his back on the floor, chest up, baby will lie face down on top. Babies have been known to sleep for long stretches in this position. They tend to drool slightly, but there's no record of a grandfather ever complaining.

• *Babies are ancient crook dwellers.*

Cain and Abel were probably the first two infants to cuddle gently in the crook of their mother's arm. Babies find security and peace nesting inside the elbow of a loving parent. They like to be fed in this position. Crook dwelling lets the baby know he belongs to someone who lovingly cares.

• *Babies long for shoulder climbing.*

After a baby finishes eating, he loves to be held up on his father's shoulder. An infant enjoys a firm hand tapping steadily on his back until he finally releases a big, resounding burp. Baby then likes to coo with contentment on his dad's broad, dependable shoulder.

Not only is it good for the baby's digestion, but Dad feels like he plays a skilled role. He let his infant burp on him.

• *Babies enjoy knee cradling.*

No nest is more complete than a baby lying on Grandmother's lap, with his head cupped in her hands.

143

Grandmother and baby find each other's eyes. Their soft voices find each other and they speak a language they both seem to understand. They connect.

Maybe Nolan will prefer different nests. But no doubt he will find favorite places, nesting with favorite people who send out the vibrations of their love.

He Better Like This Kid ...

*I*t's the cry of the wounded mother. An hour after delivery, while still in pain, we heard you issue your plaintive wail, "Gerry better like this kid because he isn't going to get another one."

And you meant it. At least for a while.

That's the common cry of mothers after the pain of labor and delivery—especially if the labor lasts many hours like yours did.

It's also a common cry if the baby weighs almost ten pounds like yours did. At the time, few mothers can imagine going through that ordeal again for anyone or any reason.

You paid the price. No doubt about it. The best gifts in life don't come free and are seldom without sacrifice. Mothers everywhere look back and remember a little of what it was like. They remember how much the cost of love really is.

This leads to another famous saying, a thought that enters every mother's mind eventually. When her child is nine or thirteen or sixteen years old and seems ungrateful, rebellious, disobedient, or otherwise normal—when the tension is tough mothers say to themselves, "After all I've done for you, you treat me like this?!"

Of course Mom is right. She went through a great deal and yet the child acts like a pirate on vacation.

But no matter how often you *feel* like saying it to your child, no matter how often you have to bite your tongue, do yourself a favor. Don't say it.

The child will simply say to himself, "Hey, I didn't ask to be born." And, of course, both of you are correct.

Love pays a price and doesn't submit a bill. Love takes the pain and doesn't try to collect on it later. Like the Bible says, "Love doesn't keep score." Love simply gives and gives and gives some more.

You might never be properly thanked by either your husband or your child. You might have to thank yourself and consider that reward enough.

It is reward enough. Through your pain came one of the most important lives in the world. You gave birth to a child, a unique person, and nothing compares with that.

God knows what you really went through. He's proud of you for your perseverance and courage. He wanted to bring another life into the world and you played the major role.

Until you receive better thanks, your own parents would like to thank you. Your pain is your own, but your gift was made to share.

Thanks for paying the price and making us glowing grandparents.

A Good Father

Many babies won't have a caring father close by. For any number of
reasons, they will grow up knowing only a
mother's love. It can work. Many mothers
have to supply most of the energy and nur-
turing for their children, and it has worked
for millions.

   Your baby has the full blessing of not
only a father in residence, but a father who
totally loves his child. Gerry overflows with
excitement and joy over his son. You could
see it in his personality as he fixed up the
nursery, painting woodwork, and picking
out a rug. You could see his caring spirit the

148

first time he held Nolan in one arm and
bathed him.

The concentration. The commitment.
The satisfaction. If Gerry ever wins the lot-
tery, it will be a letdown for him. There isn't
enough money to compare with the excitement this baby has brought into his life.

Fathers are getting a lot of bad press
lately and some of it is deserved. But not all.
There are still plenty of good fathers who
connect and follow through as proud parents.

Encourage him. Thank him. Remind
him how good he is. There is a lot of pressure on dads to give it up. Some men don't
consider it manly or productive or worth
their time to devote themselves to their
kids.

Men don't meet for coffee to talk with
other men about how they change diapers.
Not many men ask each other for tips on
how to mix formula or what to do for a crying baby at 3:00 A.M. Members of the male
species don't get much support from each
other when it comes to nursery decorum.

It's the same reason why mothers don't

usually play basketball very well. They don't while away their time shooting hoops or discussing NBA playoffs.

Nolan's dad is different. He shoots hoops, talks NBA, *and* changes diapers. He's a rare and valuable breed who can stand all the praise you can shift his way.

He's torn by a tempting career on one side (a basic need) and his love for his child on the other (just as basic). So far he's balancing them as best he can. It may always be tricky, but it looks like he'll be able to keep on an even keel.

Every couple of days tell him what a good father he is. You can say it softly, firmly, or with conviction, just be sure to say it.

If you ever had a good dad, you know how important they are.

The Oxygen Mask
Principle

he airlines have it right when the flight attendants tell you what to do when the oxygen masks drop. First, put a mask over your own face. When it's secure, and only then, reach for the second mask and place it on your child.

Too many parents fail to understand this elementary principle. If we start to put on the child's mask first, almost anything could happen. The child might begin wriggling or even panic. Seconds could turn into minutes, and the unprotected parent might begin to lose strength. As the parent weakens, he or she becomes less able to help the child. Before long neither of them has the ability to handle the situation, and they have a serious crisis on their hands.

It's easy to see how a loving parent could get into such a predicament. Her first instinct is to help her dependent infant. What parent wouldn't sacrifice his own needs to take care of her child?

The problem is, that by ignoring our own needs, we become less and less able to meet the child's. Read that sentence again.

Mothers who carefully take care of their own needs are better able to care for their children. Parents who deprive themselves, don't eat well, don't take naps, don't exercise, and don't see their friends become less able to meet an infant's real needs.

Parents who ignore the oxygen masks of life usually become short-tempered, forgetful, impatient, self-defacing, narrowminded, and less loving. They are no longer fun to be around and soon sour almost everything they touch. It really does get that bad.

152

Never make apologies for taking care of yourself. Don't apologize to your mate, your mother, your friends, your neighbor, your butcher, or your baker. And there is no need to apologize to baby. The baby gets a better balanced, kind-spirited, brighter, more understanding parent. Baby shouldn't have a complaint in the world.

When Jesus got frazzled, He took time out and took care of himself. He knew stress and strain would draw Him away from the Heavenly Father and drive Him beyond His limits. The Son of God gives us a great pattern and we would be wise to follow it.

Tell Nolan it's all right if he cries for a little while. You need to eat a few cookies, drink a glass of tea, and read part of the paper. After that you'll get back to him.

Never Fussy for Us

What are these stories we hear about our grandson being fussy? And why in the world do his parents look so tired and dragged out? Are you sure we're talking about the same child?

So far Nolan has never been grouchy for his grandparents. We've gone for stroller rides and bounced him on our knees. We've cuddled him for hours and had the little guy fall asleep in our arms. But not once, not one single time, has this delightful baby been fussy for his grandparents.

We've seemed to develop a certain charm and warmth that evidently leaves him relaxed and peaceful. He rolls his eyes, smiles, coos, and cuddles, but never does he complain. Grandparents must receive a gift from the Lord known as *good vibes*. We may not have had it when we were parents, but we certainly ooze with it now.

We admit that a part of this gift can be attributed to great timing. When Nolan starts to get hungry we pass him to his breast-feeding mother. If he messes his diaper we discreetly shift our little buddy in the direction of his attentive father. We'd like to help more with these essential services, but we didn't take the classes, read the booklets, or watch the videos.

This is the place to be. No longer the primary caregivers, we are available only during the leisure, low pressure hours. Ill-trained, we have to bail out when any real needs have to be met.

Don't talk to us about a crabby little kid. We aren't sure we can believe it.

How could a perfect grandchild like ours ever get fussy?

Not Quite Perfect

*J*t doesn't take long for some of the shine to wear off. Certainly your baby will always be awesome and special. You'll even imagine him to be better than he really is. Mothers and fathers are supposed to do that.

There is no child like yours. Hopefully you'll always be able to see the good side, the potential, the extra quality that others aren't as fully aware of. When a teacher or a neighbor or a coach gets upset, may you still see the silver lining in this wonderful child. Every child should have at least one parent, hopefully two, who really believe he is a notch above the rest.

But let's get real. Sometimes this rosy-cheeked little boy will do something rotten. And he's likely to do it before too long.

When you tell him not to splash the water, little Baby-Wonder might hit the surface one more time just to watch Mom or Dad throw a fit. After you tell Angel-Face, "Don't spit out those strained apricots," what do you think little Koochie-Woochie is going to do? That's right. And you're going to spend fifteen minutes cleaning up.

Please don't call us when you put Super-Kid on the potty for the fourth time and plead "Now you *do* something so we can get dressed and go to church" and nothing is forthcoming. Frustrated and cautious, you finally put the neatly ironed clothes on the tiny cherub. As you snap the last clasp, the Darling's sprinkler system kicks into gear and he soaks his outfit just as Daddy beeps the car horn to remind you you're running late.

When that happens (every time it happens) remind yourself that this is another lesson in redemption. Even your ideal child has fallen into imperfection. Given the opportunity to choose between good and evil, every once in a while your child will choose his own selfish ways.

Children are not innocent blank slates who are incapable of making moral decisions. At some point they'll see a window of opportunity to rattle Mom or Dad and they'll go for it.

We don't know at what age this begins. We don't know exactly under which circumstances it happens. But grandparents have no doubt it occurs.

God understands that. He sent His only Son, Jesus Christ, to earth because He understands that. God's Son redeems children, teens, parents, and grandparents who run to do wrong.

This truth need not tarnish the image of your terrific child. It only calls us to reality and explains some of the strange behavior you're going to see.

Yours is a great baby. Fortunately, your Heavenly Father is also a great God, and He sends us a Wonderful Redeemer.

All totaled it makes for a magnificent combination.